BLESSED IS THE ORDINARY

BLESSED
IS THE ORDINARY

Reflections
by
Gerhard E. Frost

WINSTON PRESS

Cover and book design by Maria Mazzara-Schade

Photographs by: Camerique – p. 40; Chuck Isaacs – p. 64; Jean-Claude Lejeune – p. viii, 16, 24, 70; Vernon Sigl – p. ii, 8, 48, 78; Rick Smolan – p. 56; Bob Taylor – p. 86; Sister Noemi Weygant – cover, p. 32.

"Be Kind," "A Difficult Art," and "The Quiet One" are reprinted from *Parish Teacher*, copyright 1978, by permission of Augsburg Publishing House. "Child Garden" and "Haunting Words" are reprinted from *Parish Teacher*, copyright 1979, by permission of Augsburg Publishing House.

All biblical quotations, except the quotation on page 47 from *The New English Bible*, are from the *Revised Standard Version of the Bible*, copyrighted 1946, 1952, © 1971, 1973.

Quotations not identified in the text:
Wisdom Knows—John 15:2
Self-Appraisal—Matthew 7:27
Child Garden—Mark 10:16
Lazarus—Luke 16:19-20
Trouble Him—Mark 5:35-43
One Generation to Another—Psalm 145:3-4
Was Jesus Less with Him?—Acts 1:23
I Love Trees—1 Peter 2:24
Praise the Lord—Psalm 148

Library of Congress Catalog Card Number: 79-55962
ISBN: 0-86683-606-3 (Previously ISBN: 0-03-056662-2)
Printed in the United States of America.

5 4 3 2

Winston Press, Inc.
430 Oak Grove
Minneapolis, Minnesota 55403

BLESSED IS THE ORDINARY

CONTENTS

PREFACE

One of the significant rewards of growing older is an increasingly multidimensional view of the world, whether one looks at a star, a child, a moment of sorrow, or a time of gladness. *Blessed Is the Ordinary* is an attempt to distill for myself and others the good that sometimes eludes us as we are caught in the pressures to achieve and succeed.

I believe that the small moment is the carrier of God's most enduring gifts and that it must not be permitted to slip away unsavored and unappreciated. It is when we fail to take a new look at situations and people close at hand that our dearest relationships suffer. And it is when we mistakenly pursue the unusual and sensational in our quest for fulfillment that we rush past the true meaning of life.

If one accepts each day as a gift from the Father's hand, one may sometimes hear a Voice softly saying, "Open it!" I invite you to share with me in these little appointments with myself as we try to unwrap the hidden beauties in an ordinary day.

Gerhard E. Frost
St. Paul, Minnesota

THESE RUDE FEET

It isn't my story,
but let me tell it:

In the Scottish highlands
a man of science knelt,
crouched in the morning dew,
the better to hold a microscope
over a heather bell.

Lost in blue traceries of exquisite design,
he saw a sun-drawn figure,
the shadow of a man.
Gazing up into a shepherd's face,
he quickly bade him look.

One long moment
the old man stood, beholding,
pierced by microscopic patterns
in the flower.
Then he spoke: "I wish
you'd never shown me that!"
"But, why?" was the surprised response.
"Because," the old man said,
gazing at two worn boots,
"these rude feet have crushed
so many of them."

These rude feet,
and this God's day,
this most resplendent hour!
Father of mercies,
give me eyes,
make me aware:
I walk in Gift today.

⚬⚬⚬

I BELIEVE

"I believe
in the holy, Christian Church,
the communion of saints . . ."

I went to church today
(a dark mood was upon me)
and everything seemed pseudo,
pseudo-Gothic, pseudo-people,
pseudo-me!
But then, there was the steeple.

I'm troubled by that steeple.

TO BE ALIVE

Only two,
a stranger to my "take-for-granteds,"
her days full of firsts,
and this was one:
my typewriter.

Seated on my lap
she stretched to reach the keys.
Her small finger found the hyphen,
striking it again and again
all across the page.

I held her high
so she could see.

"Mmm! Ants!" she said,
and looked round at me
in shared delight.
I looked, and there they were,
ants, little yellow ones,
marching single file
in their unwearying way.
There they were, also for me,
made free to image with her
in her world of glad discovery.

A few more seconds
of clicking and admiring
and she was on her way,
filled with the satisfactions
of success.

Measured by my standard,
touch-key grown-upness,
I would call it failure,
but what is it to succeed?
Isn't it to be alive,
to see more than there is,
to hear more than is said,
to be more than I am?

WISDOM KNOWS

". . . and every branch
that does bear fruit he prunes . . ."

Wenatchee, Washington:
I watch the apple harvest,
ruby-red and sun-gold,
treasuring the lessons I learn.

Close-clinging clusters,
fruit touching fruit,
must feel the violent hand
in early youth.
Where there are three two must go,
two out of three, three out of four.

Ruthless waste?
No, wisdom knows, and has seen
the late disaster of the overburdened tree,
the clinging fruit, hiding the parasite
which devastates and destroys.

Is it so in faith's orchard, too,
that no unpruned branch
can bear the strain,
be trusted with too much success,
that thinning must go on
against lives too lush
and parasites of pride and self?

Faith trusts the One
who holds the knife,
the saw, the hook,
and sees wisdom
in love's violent hand.

❧❧❧

SELF-APPRAISAL

"And great was the fall of it,"
Jesus said.
He spoke of a house,
the one that was built on sand.

You see, it was an important house.

And I am important.
And you. We're somebodies!
What proof, you ask?
This, that our fall was great.

For Jesus it meant the Cross.
This is our claim to greatness;
it is the reason he died.

Don't be afraid to say "great,"
and count yourself in;
only add the word, "sinner."

HIS WAY FOR ME

The profoundest thing
one can say of a river
is that it's on its way to the sea.

The deepest thought
one can think of a person
is that he or she is a citizen of eternity.

Moments and years,
years and moments,
pass like sea-bent streams.
And I? I'm carried by the current
of an all-possessing Love.
I'm on my way, God's way for me,
so let it be.

SCIENCE LECTURE

I held her warm hand
as we walked in the park
at sunset, by the lake.

My mind "recorded"
her kindergarten lecture
as she chattered on:
"See the 'flections?
That's the fishes' world.
And do you know?
The sun is always shining
and the night is always nighting,
because, you see,
the world is round!"

I've paid tuition for less.

HEAVEN-SENT

The world was new that day in May,
dew-drenched, sun-bathed,
all nature saying "Hi"
to me.

But I didn't hear.

Sheathed in despair,
(for my news was bad),
tuned in to my lone self,
I couldn't hear.

Just then a friend
fell into step with me.
"It's great to be alive," he said,
expecting my doxological response.

A muffled grunt
was my confession of faith,
all I could muster then.

But now
I see him, heaven-sent,
sent to walk with me,
to be the Word made flesh,
to be the prompter
of my forgotten lines
from God.

"We are buried, therefore,
with Christ, by baptism, unto death,
so that as he was raised from the dead
by the glory of the Father
we, too, might walk in newness of life."

It is, indeed,
great to be alive. Alleluia!

HER LANGUAGE

Christmas Eve,
late afternoon,
(I believe I was seven),
and mother, bless her,
was making something special.
Instead of the traditional
jello, whipped cream, and bananas,
she was baking a towering pie!

I stood at her elbow,
as small boys always will,
as she peeked for a moment
through the partly open oven door.

Perfect!
the meringue just right
in color and consistency;
the moment had arrived.

Carefully, so cautiously,
she drew it out,
when suddenly
a slip of those sure hands,
and a capsized tower
slithered across the floor,
never to be a pie again.

And mother, no weeper,
(I could count the times),
covered her face with her apron
and cried.

I was outraged
that God could let it happen
because no one—
but no one—
cries on Christmas Eve!

Why did she do it,
prepare this gift
for hungry little gluttons?
(Jello was enough!)
I know: it was her language
for telling us
that we were special.

More than sixty years have come and gone,
sixty Christmases,
and I remember that one
and its gift of tears.

THE SENT ONE

I remember being sent;
it made me
ten feet tall.

How dignifying
to walk in borrowed prestige
down that winding road
to the country store.
I carried a note,
not in my handwriting, of course,
because I couldn't write;
but I could scribble.

I never scribbled on that note.

And I was careful,
so careful lest it fall in the dirt.
I was content just to carry it.

To be sent
is an exercise in being third.
First, there's the sender;
second, the one to whom you're sent;
and then, you, the sent one.
Any two without the other won't do.

"He called to him the twelve,"
the scriptures say,
"and began to send them two by two . . .
and he charged them. . . ."
He called them, he sent them, he charged them.
What an honor to be carriers of his love!

❧❧❧

TAKE, EAT

"Take . . . eat":
Our Host's invitation,
his gentle command;
he asks us not to stand aloof
until we comprehend.
He wants no wallflowers;
all must join the dance.

"O, Lamb of God, I come,"
a babe in understanding,
breast-fed on your unending care.
"Incomprehensible love,
I trust, I take, I eat,
I rest in You."

I LOVE TREES

"He himself bore our sins in his body
on the tree . . ."

I love trees
and respect them, too—
respect them for their uniqueness
and individual characters.

You can read a tree.
Each is a story
of triumph and disaster.

I respect trees for their silences
and am fascinated by their sounds.
I respect them for their patience
and stand in awe of their reminders
of my own mortality.
I know, when I plant a tree,
that it will outlive me.

I love trees
because they die so honestly
and stand naked and revealed.

I resonate to Albert Schweitzer's words
to a disheartened friend,
"Say not that there is nothing beautiful
in the world. There is still
the shape of a leaf and the tremor of a tree."

I love birches,
graceful saints of the woodland,
wearing white halos in moonlight and sunlight,
wind and rain.
On quiet days they whisper secrets
known only to the forest,
and leave me wondering still.

I love poplars, common and ordinary,
their leaves gossiping in the wind—
small talk, unfestive and everyday.
I love willows, human and yielding,
and evergreens, proud and unafraid,
impervious to the changing seasons.
I love them all, the scraggiest jack pine,
the towering tamarack, the age-old redwood
and sequoia.

I love maples for their painful autumn beauty.
I love cottonwoods,
messy, unshapely mammoths,
standing beleaguered against the hills,
perhaps the best expression of who I am.

My love embraces elm and basswood,
ash and rosewood,
celebrates all differences
of shape and color and leaf,
and even aroma, fresh-cut or crackling
in a winter fire.

I love trees for gifts:
shade and shelter,
fruits and nuts and flowers.

But most of all,
I love oaks.
In winter silhouette and summer glory
they tell their story—
express the character
wrought by weather's chastening discipline.

I love the Tree.
I love the tree that held the Son of God
and Son of Man,
who gave himself for me.

"I give thanks unto thee, O Lord,
Holy Father, Almighty, Everlasting God
who on the Cross didst give salvation
unto mankind; that whence death arose,
thence life also might rise again:
and that he who by a tree once overcame,
might also by a Tree be overcome."

THE CORNER

A hot and humid silence,
all nature coiled to strike,
and Sheba, heaven help her,
cowering in her corner
and growling at the thunder.

I know her well,
our golden retriever,
know, too, that like her kind
and all humans,
she's fiercest when she's most afraid.
And I know something
of our trembling hearts,
the sullen defiance
within myself and others.

Why this fierce unkindness, Lord,
toward you and one another?
Forgive us,
and perfect our feeble trust,
lest, spent and weary,
we waste ourselves in growling our defiance,
each in a dreary corner.

WE WON

I remember a moment long ago
in a small-town restaurant.

We'd played a basketball game—
played away from home and won,
and were in a celebrative mood.
I was fourteen, and not very good,
nor was our team, and this made victory
sweeter still.

As we crowded into a booth
I jauntily said, "Well, we won!"
Quick as the flash of a knife
came the remembered words:
"What do you mean, we?
You didn't play!"

I can't forget the words
or the one who spoke them,
but I can turn to other words,
sounding in my soul.
My Lord says, "This do
in remembrance of me."
Baptized into the death of Christ
I die in him to rise again.
With no part in the victory
I'm still invited to say,
"We won!"

CHILD GARDEN

"And he took them in his arms
and blessed them . . ."

When I think of teaching
I see an arm around a child,
for teaching is embrace.

But without the throb of love
an arm is nothing.
Children sense caring
and know unfailingly
when an arm is dead.

We blossom under praise
like flowers in sun and dew;
we open, we reach, we grow.

Teaching is a look, a word,
a smile, a gesture,
as thought lights up thought
and knowledge brings new joy;
it is an ear, an eye, a hand,
and sometimes even a tear,
but most of all,
an arm around a child.

JUST THINKING

November thirteenth:
Today I passed through Bennetville.
To tell the truth,
I didn't know there was a Bennetville
until today.

Passed through,
did I say?
But how can one pass through
a one-store town,
its only dog,
a springer spaniel,
sitting forlornly
in the cold?

I guess I didn't pass through;
I just sped by.

I've been thinking:
Why wasn't I born
a springer spaniel
in Bennetville?

SILENT THINGS

I like to think of silent things:
sunbeams and stars,
meadows and mountains,
rocks and fields,
and especially winding paths.

Silent happenings—
like dawn breaking
and evening coming on,
summer fading into autumn,
April deferring to May,
planted seed
and Truth well taught—
silent things that won't be forced
and can't be hurried.

God's Spirit broods
over silent things,
movements of life
and ministries of love.

There is healing in thinking
of silent things.

HAPPY BIRTHDAY

A great teacher.
His name is Graham,
and he lives in a cluster
of little shadows,
mostly nine-year-olds.
They love him, and follow,
and wait, and wonder,
confident that their
curiosity will be fed.
Now a book, now a picture,
now a field trip or a story—
always something worth
waiting and working for.
Yes, a great teacher.

But when I think of Graham
I want to laugh, not
in ridicule, but in admiration
and remembrance.
I remember Graham's birthday.
We had gathered to celebrate
with cake and candles,
cards and conversation.

One card, in childish script, read:
"You are a great, good teacher,
but mean. Happy birthday.
The Fourth Grade."

"But mean?"
They loved him!
No one truly thought him mean.
They were saying:
"You are good to us;
you make it all so interesting;
we really think it's fun.
But thank you for helping us
to outgrow our need of you.
Thank you for not crippling us
by running our errands for us,
the bracing errands of the mind."

WHERE IS HE NOW?

Time has passed, but I can't forget
one nameless face.

I saw him for most of a year—
at least three times a week—
as I waited for Jersey buses
in New York's 167th Street station.
Almost always he stumbled
along the waiting line,
extending a grimy and unsteady hand.

But this day was different,
a Sunday in late spring,
the station deserted except for three,
the man, my wife, and me.
Less disheveled, more at peace,
he didn't beg, but sat serenely
in the unused shoeshine chair.

A woman entered, perhaps a grandmother,
with a comely child in springtime dress.
To our surprise, she turned and said,
"Please watch her while I telephone."

We watched the child by the telephone booth;
I watched him, too,
the man in the shoeshine chair,
saw his lips move as he talked to himself
and gazed at the waiting one.
Then, fumbling in his pocket
for a cherished treasure,
he drew it forth, a very special thing—
a rosary!

Hesitantly, tentatively, he approached her,
the wee one waiting unafraid.
He placed his offering about her neck,
then, with a high ceremony
and deep contentment,
he resumed his place in the chair.

Why did he do it? I've asked myself
through passing years, Where is he now?
Who was he, that derelict on 167th Street?
Was he—is he—a saint, I wonder,
nearer than many who scorned him
to the Kingdom of God's Grace?

FRIGHTENED

I'm always frightened
whenever I see strident arrogance
walk the streets,
especially in one I love,
for I know that sorrow
walks close behind.

❧

LAZARUS

"There was a rich man . . .
and at his gate lay a poor man
named Lazarus . . ."

Lazarus, O Lazarus,
you—
you at my door,
you're controversial,
do you know that?
Please find some other door.

We quarrel—
at church, I mean—
we fight over you.

O, we argue some,
and not so little,
over other things,
but, Lazarus,
these things are safe,
so safe compared with you.

The trouble,
Lazarus,
is that you're too near.
Half a continent away,
or, better yet,
a hemisphere,
we can abide you,
but your presence
repels, convicts,
enrages, frightens.
You leave no hiding place.

Lazarus, please,
please find another door.
And please, Lazarus,
leave us your dogs
to lick our larger sores.

THE TASTE IN YOUR MOUTH

He's a man of many skills
and much good will,
this north-woods carpenter,
friend of every do-it-yourselfer
who can't quite do it
and must call on Bob.
He has worked these many years
to the rhythms and melodies
of the lake-lands
under whispering birches
and towering pines.

One day, so they tell it,
a friend—a city man—said,
"Since work is kind of scarce
why don't you come to the city, Bob?"
And Bob is said to have answered,
"Well, what have you got?
Your wife, your family, your home
and a taste in your mouth.
And I'm not quite sure
of the taste in my mouth
if I moved down there."

That taste in your mouth,
what is it? Is it serenity,
at oneness with self and others,
contentment, and a sense of life well lived?
Or is it all of these,
and a growing awareness of God,
His eternal goodness
and daily care?

✧✧✧

THE ACTION

". . . he went about
doing good . . ."

The trouble with Jesus?
He was such a wastrel—
a squanderer, of time,
I mean.

He just wasn't where the action is.

I'd never have traveled with him;
why, we'd never have made it on time!

If Jesus were here, in the flesh, I mean,
he'd miss the action every time,
what with avoiding freeways
and staying on country roads.
Why, he'd arrive at every three-day convention
about noon of the third day,
and at every two-hour meeting
just in time for our Lord's Prayer.

Always late, with time to throw away
on frightened children, blind folks,
and the demon-possessed.
Even time to pet the dogs? Perhaps.
(Though I've heard they were despised
where Jesus lived.)

Time for sunsets, bird-watchings,
child-blessings, leper-cleansings,
and every lost cause, but not for the action—
a most inefficient man—
unless, of course, he was the action,
and still is!

ALL FLIGHTS CANCELED

"All flights canceled;
the airport is now closed."

Snowbound in an airport,
sixteen of us, wanting to be in Portland.
No longer strangers,
but one in a common frustration
and disappointment.
No longer in charge,
our psyches wounded and unwilling
to acknowledge complete dependence,
we struggle, we resist—
lash out in mutual anger
at falling into others' hands.

"They," we say, "they
can't do this to us!"
But they can, they do,
they've done it—
the invisible "they."

But one among us,
one small person,
roams free.

With so much to celebrate,
so much carpet and color,
and so much coordination,
he runs and rolls and jumps;
he sings, he shouts,
and in his smiles and songs
we find our medicine.

Is it always so—
the spirit of the child within
leading us to relinquish ourselves
into strong, invisible hands—
hands which sustain all flights
and hold us in that hour of hours
when the word is stark and stern:
all flights canceled?

LOVE CHEATS

I remember my mouthy days,
my dazzling debates
with mom and dad.

Like a winner,
confidently I'd argue,
condescendingly I'd instruct,
tolerantly I'd repeat,
patiently I'd wait,
until, without a moment's warning,
one of them would say,
"You know, we love you!"

"Foul!" I'd yearn to cry,
and I'd want out.
They'd struck so hard—
and below the belt.

Love cheats.
It always does;
there's no defense.

SATURDAY MORNING

Lord, you know,
I've been straightening my desk,
and I needn't tell you
I'm a piler, not a filer,
and if I were a filer
I'd still lose things—
alphabetically, I mean.

So, Lord,
as you once brooded
over primeval chaos
let your Spirit brood today
over this clutter
which is my life,
lest I lose myself
and you,
the Eternal Best.

THE QUIET ONE

I remember the quiet one.
My friend told me about him,
this very quiet man.
He confessed he'd judged,
yes, misjudged,
misread the quietness
as lack of depth.
A bore, he thought,
with nothing much to share.

Then, unexpectedly, one day
the quiet one said:
"You know, one is only limited by oneself
in the beauty one sees
when one goes for a walk."

Searching words,
words to live by,
words from one misjudged.
Lord, help us to listen and wait
lest we pass by the "quiet in the land."

PLAYGROUND

She loves costumes,
and drama even more;
grandma, bless her, had helped her
with her gown, so today,
with a crown of leaves to complete it,
she was "the princess of nature."
That made grandma the queen
and me the king!

And so we began,
royalty and I:
"Fair maiden," I said,
"will you live in the castle?"
"O, yes, in the highest room."
"And will there be sky,
the bluest of the blue?"
"Yes, and water that sparkles as it flows!"

Then, abruptly,
and to my surprise,
she flitted up the stairway.
I wondered, "What's happening now?"
But quickly she reappeared,
her face twisted with anguish.

"Oh, they haven't made my room!
The emeny, I mean the emeny—
well, I can't say the word, but you know,
those bad snow people—
they won't let them."

"Then, they shall go to the dungeon,"
I, the king, decreed.
"And, fair one, how long shall they remain?"
"Ninety-seven years!" she said.
"And then, if they are not good?"
"Ninety-seven more!"

At this moment,
forgetting my role,
I exclaimed, "Wow!"
Quick as a flash
she rescued us,
"Indeed, wow, indeed!"

A little child shall lead them
into the treasure house
of laughter.

ONE GENERATION TO ANOTHER

"Great is the Lord, and greatly to be praised,
and his greatness is unsearchable.
One generation shall laud thy works to another,
and shall declare thy mighty acts."

Kabekona. Magic word.
To me, two decades of family,
a clear, blue lake,
and a woodland cabin;
more than twenty babies
(cousins in the clan),
"leaving father and mother,"
always to return to this place held dear.

When I think of Kabekona
I remember
the words of one of the cousins,
now eighteen years old.
Addressing his aunt, he asked,
"Do you know what I like best about Kabekona?"
"No, what?" she answered.
"We're all in the same room!" he said.

"All in the same room."
An exciting description of education
as cross-generational sharing,
hearing and telling old family stories
which flow into the Story, older still.

WE WALK BY FAITH

She spoke of her church in anger—
fire in her eyes:
"Believe me, the churches that are growing
know how to draw people in;
they give them what they want,
answers, full and final answers!"

"Well," I answered, weakly, "doesn't that
cater to the weakness of wanting things too neat?"
I sensed that she wasn't satisfied.
I know now what I should have said:
"With all those answers,
where's the need for faith?"

To traffic in simple answers—
isn't that promising too much?
Is this respect for Truth—
Truth, always unfolding,
deepening and reaching beyond?
Where *is* the life of faith unless one follows
where one cannot see and has never been?

I UNDERSTAND

I used to think
that imagination
is just for "tripping,"
going places, wild places,
meeting people, wild people,
and for setting goals.

Now I understand
that imagination
is for *loving*,
for wearing others' shoes,
getting into others' skins.

How can one care
if one can't imagine,
can't see and feel
from the other side?

Imagination is for caring,
serving, helping with the invisible load.
Imagination, the mind's pleasure cruise,
but the heart's workroom.

WAS JESUS LESS WITH HIM?

"Two names were put forward:
Joseph, who was known as Barsabbas . . .
and Matthias. . . .
They drew lots
and the lot fell to Matthias,
who was then assigned a place
among the twelve apostles."

Joseph lost.
He lost in the drawing;
the chips just fell that way.

I wonder,
did he take it hard,
had he hoped and planned,
this man with so little Bible ink?
Did he congratulate Matthias,
then secretly hate?

Was Jesus less with him
than with the other?
Did Joseph's wife fan the flame
of smoldering bitterness,
or love and affirm
this loser of hers?

His name was "put forward"—
I'll wager Joseph was a winner,
too wise to spend himself in hating.

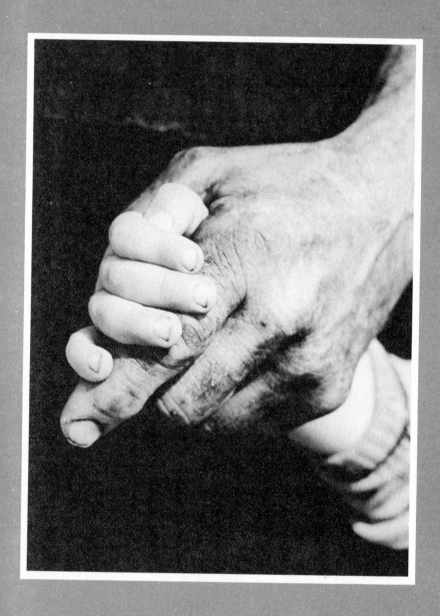

HEZEKIA 6:14

"The reason mountain climbers
are tied together
is to keep the sane ones from going home."

I don't know who said it,
or when, or where,
but I've chuckled over it,
thought about it, and quoted it, too.

With a mountain of mercy behind me
and a mountain of mission ahead,
I need you, my sister, my brother,
I need to be tied to you,
and you need me, too.

We need each other
(the Holy Christian Church)
to keep from bolting,
fleeing in panic, and returning
to the "sanity" of unbelief.

Wise words, whoever said them;
I've placed them in my "bible";
they are my Hezekia 6:14.

THE GIFT

Nineteen-twenty-seven:
Well I remember the long winter
and days of tired waiting.
I was seventeen,
at home with my sister, six,
while mother kept bedside vigil
as our father's life
slowly and painfully
ebbed away.

Hard days,
today a memory, but more,
of the giving of the great gift.

He'd given much, and now,
mind and spirit weary,
body spent and broken,
one thing remained: a thought,
for me a life-directing gift.

I wasn't there;
he wouldn't have known me;
he knew no human face,
not even hers, my mother said.

He couldn't find words
to speak his crying needs;
yet two remained:
"Praeke evangeliet! Praeke evangeliet!"
Hour after hour, day after day,
in that, his final week:
"Preach the Gospel! Preach the Gospel!"

Blessed residue,
two words, one thought,
expressive of the habit
of one spent life—
to us the last, the best,
the greatest gift.

AIRBORNE

Lord of the airways,
I go to meet you
in Great Falls.
Flying time: three hours.

The blue above is yours,
the brown below,
the white, the gray
of floating cloud.
You run ahead, you follow after,
you dwell within.

You are everywhere for good.

O God,
you are around me
and above me,
and beneath me.
You wait upon me
in your Holy Word.

The wind blows
where it wills:
your Truth will not be bound
since grace is everywhere.

WHERE THOUGHT BREAKS DOWN

"You know, we're here."
"Yeah, we exist.
Isn't that something?"

Overheard from a conversation
of two eighteen-year-olds
as they painted our house
(they didn't know).

Only the smallest snippet,
nothing more,
but enough,
enough to send us all
to pondering the poignancy
of the fact
that we *are*!

We may go further,
but we can't go deeper,
for it brings us
straight to the A
of the alphabet of mystery,
the "In the beginning God" moment,
where thought breaks down
and yields to prayer.

TROUBLE HIM

"Your daughter is dead . . .
why trouble the Teacher. . . ?"

"Dead":
It was like the slamming of a door,
so they talked hopeless talk.
"Why trouble the Teacher?"
they said.

Teacher?
But Jesus is more,
so hope knocks softly at faith's door.
"Trouble him," she says,
"trouble him, O grieving one,
with the trouble he craves,
for he loves you!"

"Not dead, but sleeping," Jesus said.
They laughed at him,
as they always have.

But Jairus didn't laugh.
He'd heard, had listened
to hope-filled words:
"Do not fear,
only believe."

Parting laughers from believers,
Jesus went in, and it happened,
the unthinkable, the unheard-of.
Unveiling his Lordship
over life and death, he said,
"Give her something to eat."

~~~

DOCK TALK

God, our Father,
let's sit together
here on the dock
and watch your sunset—
I mean, our sunset.

You like it, too—
the sunset?
You made it;
you want it to be.

You like me?
You made me.
You want me to be!

ALIVE AGAIN

Today I left the freeway
to meander and explore,
experience the winding sideroads,
and I'm a person again.

On the freeways of the mind
generalizations hurry by,
and amid stampeding statistics,
person starves for person.
Crowding, nudging, jostling,
there's little touching
and not much meeting there.

I thank God for freeways—
my world is bigger now—
but I'll not do my living there.
Solitude demands friendship,
lest it turns to loneliness
and makes one callous
to man's inhumanity to man.

When I think of teaching
I treasure the "asides,"
the little country roads
where I slow down
and let the other person in.

OLD RECIPE: 1920

Take catechisms, Bibles, and songbooks,
dog-eared and tattered;
mix well with children
in a red brick schoolhouse
beside a church and country store;
let there be a dusty road
winding through woodland pastures
to a deep valley, a creek
fed from a clear, cool mill pond,
and a hundred hidden springs;
let there be a bend and a bridge
and a swimming hole.

And let there be games,
and wrestling, loitering, talking,
laughing—and a very little crying;
and let there be candy corn, jelly beans,
vanilla creams, and peanuts in the shell.
Then don't forget wild things along the way:
cranes, crows, quail, and bobolinks;
woodchucks, weasels, skunks, and rabbits;
and wild berries—strawberries, gooseberries,
raspberries, and june-berries
for going to and coming from.

Then find Harry and Oscar,
Levi, Jolly, Jack—
and me, of course.
Fetch a teacher,
ask the Holy Spirit, invite Jesus,
invoke our Father,
and what do you have?
A lot of "What is meant by this?",
"Not with silver or gold . . .",
"Not by my own reason or strength . . .",
"This is most certainly true."

What do you have?
Six old men?
No, a recipe
for Christ's promise fulfilled:
"Lo, I am with you always,
even to the end of the age."

IF RIVERS COULD REBEL

If rivers could speak,
and if they could rebel,
would they say:
We want no banks,
no shape, nothing to hem us in?
And if they could have their way
they'd never be rivers, only swamps,
and they would miss the sea.

If I could have my way
when I sullenly say,
I want no higher Will,
no god but me,
I'd never know Him, or you,
or our vast humanity.

I'd lose myself
in the swamp of "little me."

HAUNTING WORDS

When I think of teaching
I recall another teacher's words:
"If you can't say it simply,
you either don't understand it
or you don't believe it."

Haunting words,
but are they true?

Yes, when you believe,
and try to say what you believe,
knowledge weds wisdom
and heart-language is born.
Little words, feeling words,
sturdy, simple words,
strong-backed servants
emerge to do Truth's bidding,
for simplicity is the vocabulary
of depth.

Haunting words,
disturbing words,
but true.

I WASN'T AFRAID

"And I wasn't scairt—
I wasn't afraid to die!"

He said it as one who'd returned
from the outer spaces
in the journey of the soul.
And he had.

He said it as one who'd tasted
and tested, and settled something,
as one who'd been found
by the Father in a most
unfatherly place.
And he had.

It happened while he worked alone
in a city gravel pit.
A sudden collapse, a fall,
a tangle of cables,
and no one to hear his cries.
Two hours he hung, head down,
suffered in that forsaken place
until he was rescued,
but our Father found him there.

Another hung suspended,
alone upon his cross.
He cried to God, cried
in that most unfatherly place:
"My God, my God, why
have you forsaken me?"
And prayed, "Father,
into your hands
I commend my spirit."

And because he cried,
and prayed,
and died,
there is today no God-forsaken place,
or moment, or man,
or woman, or child—
no God-forsaken person anywhere.

Not afraid to die?
I need not cry,
but only pray,
"Father, into your hands . . ."

THE BETTER TO KNOW

Lord,
you stab me
with the beauties
of your world.

Yesterday it happened again.
I listened to birdcalls
in treetops, bushes, and bending grass,
walked barefoot in the morning dew,
eavesdropped on concerts and conversations
of the summer woodland.

Lord, prick me
with rose petal, sunset, and dawn;
assail me with sight and smell and sound;
torment me with shape and texture and taste.
Lord, make me bleed,
the better to know,
the greater to be,
the more to find myself in You.

THE SEED

We swim together,
my granddaughter and I
(she's eight),
so I telephoned
on this warm August day:
"Will you be ready when I come?"
And she was.

As I turned the corner
I spied her from a distance,
bright orange bathing suit,
curly dark head bent over a book,
intent on her reading.

The sound of the horn is usually sufficient
to bring her bounding toward me,
but not today.
Slowly, like one interrupted in a dream,
open book in hand, she came.

"Oh, granddaddy," she exclaimed,
"I'm reading the most beautiful book!"
"What is it?" I asked.
The Wind in the Willows," she replied.
"That is beautiful," I said.
"I know quite a lot about it."

"I don't understand all the words,"
she continued, "but I like their sound,
like 'full-fed river.'"
"Oh, yes," I answered,
"and it means that hundreds
of brooks and creeks and smaller rivers
keep feeding the big river,
sending it toward the ocean."

"And what does i-n-s-a-t-i-a-b-l-e spell?"
"Insatiable," I said.
And she: "Listen to this,
'the insatiable sea', isn't
that beautiful?"
And we talked about its meaning.

"And don't you like the sound of
The Wind in the Willows?" she continued.
"Don't you think it's a little like
'the last of the light of the sun
that had died in the west
still lived for one song more
in a thrush's breast'?"
(lines from Robert Frost
which we'd struggled to memorize
a few days before)

A seed had been sown, I knew,
the seed of appreciation and love
for the good, the beautiful,
and the true.

And I was glad.

～～～

BE KIND

"You know, mom,
your world is pretty nice
compared to going out to recess."

Startling words from one
in fourth grade;
they surprised her mother
as they do me.
They tell us that we
can't see clearly
the "worlds" of one another,
that threatening things
appear so tame when
faced by someone else.

They tell us, too,
to look and listen.
They say: "Be kind."

LET THEM IN

Teaching is knowledge shared
in the risks of self-disclosure.
And I hear the voice of Martin Buber:
"Withhold not yourself."

Once and for all
the Word became person,
and we beheld his glory—
saw the face of reality,
life as it is intended to be.

We learn through a chain
of little incarnations.
I follow this thought backward
to the Christ who was,
and forward to the Christ who is,
source and content of Truth,
he who never withheld himself
that in his self-giving we, too, may live.

I ask:
does he find a person,
a self-sharing person,
in me?

I LOVE A TREE

I have a love affair,
a very private thing,
with one familiar oak.
It grows ten paces from our door,
massive and strong and tall.

This tree comforts and encourages,
calls to me as I leave for my next class:
"If I can grow from a buried acorn,
forgotten by one absentminded squirrel,
perhaps you, too, an absentminded professor,
may say something today, and then forget,
something that may plant an oak
in the forests of humanity."

So, I believe in acorns;
this is a part of my teacher's creed.

Unique among our trees,
this oak speaks.
It speaks of power and age,
and deep, deep roots;
but, most of all, it tells of suffering,
in its most stark and visible feature:
no major branch grows toward the east!

In some harsh moment of a long and testing past
my tree has felt disaster,
such force of tragedy that it must live its years
without the slightest symmetry.

Distorted, bent, unyielding in every wind
it wrenches at its roots,
but holds and stands to greet the dying winds
that mark the end of every storm.
This special tree,
I name it Job.

~~~

SOMETHING BETTER

I remember a day
when I was five,
the day the nursery man
came to our door.

I stood at his elbow
as he wrote my father's order
for shrubs and fruit trees.
Suddenly, surprising me,
he turned to a picture
of a rose bush in brilliant color
and said, "I'm going to give you that."

Delighted,
I ran to the kitchen,
returning in a moment
with shears in hand.
Now it was his turn
to be surprised, as he said,
"Oh, no, not the picture;
I'll give you a live rose bush,
and, if you care for it,
there will be roses every summer!"

I was disappointed.

True to my immaturity,
I'd rather have a trinket today
than a treasure tomorrow.

How often God says "No"
when our good is less than his best.
How many of our prayers trail far behind
God's perfect plan for us.
We ask for dead things
when he is in the business of Life.

We can't assess prayer
from this narrow chimney corner
of a world. God alone
has the total view.

A DIFFICULT ART

"But they don't do things perfect
in fourth grade!"
I remember this vehement protest
of one who felt she'd been robbed.

Her teacher had helped,
and now her father,
both overhelping
as we sometimes do
from our grown-up's world.

A difficult art in helping
is knowing when to stop.

Living with the young
we have it in our power
to rob them,
remove them,
and even destroy
by overhelp,
all in the name of love.

Dear Lord, all-wise and good,
protect them,
protect them from us,
who love them.

DEARLY BELOVED

My friend says,
"We speak too often
of the poverty and meanness
of the Holy Christian Church,
too seldom of her riches."

He must be right.
There is much pettiness,
meanness, and hypocrisy
in you and me,
and we are the church,
but what can be more
irrelevant?

You don't belong
because of me,
nor I because of you,
but you and I belong
to Christ!

Why spend ourselves
and waste God's time
in partnered floggings of ourselves
and others?
Why wallow in self-evident wrong?
We are not bastard orphans;
we are the "dearly beloved"—
our heavenly nickname!

RUDY

I remember Rudy,
kindest and shyest of men,
the first of our class
to be taken by death.
But he left a legacy
which I treasure still.

Alone in a distant land,
so they tell it,
alone among black sisters and brothers
and stricken to the point of dying,
he spoke to a servant-child:
"Don't play with the Word of God."

Yes, Rudy, I know,
know better because of you:
The Word is many things,
bread to the hungry,
light to the blind,
rest to the weary—
the way in the wilderness,
an anchor in the storm,
a sword for the battle.

But you keep speaking, Rudy.
"Respect the Word," you say,
"for, like wind and fire and water,
it has power, and Truth is never a toy!"

CHRISTMAS LESSON

Christmas Eve,
everything in highest key,
the dinner, the tree, the songs and gifts;
but now the hour was late,
with only grown-ups left.
But then the best of all,
that round of visits to all four beds,
the ritual inventory on Christmas Eve.

There he lay,
our child of seven Christmases,
dreams of celebration
reflected on his happy face.

But what was this,
protruding from the blanket?
Two new gloves—with rabbit fur, no less!

Soundly he slept in these,
his newest gifts.

"You teach us well, my son,"
I said, "teach me, your grown-up dad,
(too big for grace sometimes),
the Christmas lesson: how gifts
are believed, received, possessed.
I salute you, child,
you great receiver from our Father's hand."

NEVER SAY ONLY

"We have only five loaves here
and two fish . . ."

Almost nothing,
hardly worth counting,
but Jesus was there.

Loved child,
you feel forgotten,
naked, hungry, sick,
with nothing to remember
and less to expect,
but Jesus is here.
Your Father is King.

Therefore,
never say only.

ENOCH

Advent, 1977.
A cruelly frigid morning
for a men's breakfast,
but I had agreed to speak,
so, straightening my halo,
I went.

I walked briskly over crisp snow,
feeling heroic and thinking
of what I would say.

We arrived at the same moment,
my friend and I, from opposite directions.
"Good morning!" I said.
Seeming almost startled,
he replied, "Oh, good morning.
I was just finishing my prayer,
my walking prayer, I call it,
and I didn't forget to include you."

Then he confided his little habit
(today he'd practiced it
those eight cold blocks)
of praying for people along the way,
for himself and whoever came to mind.

A "walking prayer."
"His name isn't Enoch," I thought,
"but it might have been."

WELCOME

What joy to leapfrog over the years
and alight at the castle of memory,
the old house, the big house
with its four wood-burning stoves
and its big black hard-coal heater!

I'd creep into my father's study,
sometimes to find him deep in concentration;
I'd sense "no trespassing,"
but not really, not absolutely,
so I'd curl up quietly in a corner
behind the potbellied stove.

I'd wait, and always it happened:
he'd look up and smile at me,
and I would smile,
and heart-warmth filled the air.

There was welcome there.

"He's glad I'm born—to him,"
I'd say to my luxuriating self.
"And I'm glad, too, just cozy-glad to be,
to belong—to him."

Great Father of us all,
to be, to sit in your smile
is faith's delight beyond all words
of thanks and praise; accept my silence then.
Amen.

ENTRUST IT ALL TO HIM

He lives within my city,
so I'm told—
a little boy-child
who really wants to know!
Offended, asking, wondering,
hurt by all the grown-ups
who won't tell.
He's sure they know.

His question:
"What's the last number?"
There must be one,
like the last letter—
everyone knows it's Z—
but, what's the last number?

Ah, child,
you are my little brother.
I, too, have puzzled
and do wonder;
I hurt with you;
I've always wished to know.

Infinity, eternity:
I borrow from their vastness
and am a borrower still.

Each asking child
is brother, sister,
to every child that's been.
But, peace to you,
little brother, sister,
if we could know the last number
our God would be no God,
no shelter for our creature-life.

Infinity, eternity:
entrust it all to him
and be at rest.

PRAISE THE LORD

"Praise the Lord!
Praise the Lord from the heavens!
. . . fire and hail . . ."

We sat together,
this tall man and a tiny child,
before the fireplace.
Enthralled with this, her first,
and looking up at me,
she said, "It's clapping!"

I would have said,
"It's crackling,"
and so would you—
victims of the dulling years—
but who is right?
Who has really heard?
Can fire praise by crackling?

No, she's the one
who has found the word.
Indeed, it's clapping.
"Praise the Lord!"

GOING ON

In the long shadows of late November
we stood at the grave of one beloved
as husband, father, friend,
and I overheard soft-spoken words,
not meant for me,
but words to remember.

The moment had arrived,
that time that comes
in every hour of grief,
the moment for going on.
It was then that she,
the daughter and the only child,
spoke words intended just
for her mother: "Well, mama?"

Two softly spoken words,
nothing more, and yet so much
in meaning and in courage,
much with which to turn together
toward a future with a different face,
words of hope and love, great love,
for we honor those who've taught us
to face forward by going on.

LET US GIVE THANKS

Let us give thanks this moment:
for the sturdy fact of God's continuing love,
for mercies which go before us
and follow after us,
for those free gifts
which cost God so much.

Let us give thanks:
for memory and expectation,
for the good that we have known
and know today in Jesus Christ,
for the Spirit's brooding presence
in our nights and in our days.

Let us give thanks:
for pleasures which comfort
and pains which force our growth
and keep us at the Shepherd's side,
for deep meanings revealed
and mysteries, mercifully concealed,
for the image of God within us,
the capacity to inquire and adore.

Let us give thanks for one another,
for just being together,
for differences which complement and complete,
for gifts which enrich
and disagreements which challenge,
for our oneness in Christ.

Let us give thanks for melody and mirth,
for rhythm and beat,
for the repeated and the common,
for the ever-unfolding,
and for senses with which to respond.

And let us give thanks for Someone to thank.